lonely planet KIDS

101 THINGS
to do on a
WALK

Written by Kait Eaton

Illustrated by Vivian Mineker

Contents

Explore and discover 10

Activities and things to do 36

Get ready for walking adventures!

Whether you're heading out on a pre-planned hike, or a simple spur-of-the-moment stroll to get a bit of fresh air, this book will boost the fun factor and make any walk more entertaining, interesting and enjoyable!

Read on to discover 101 different ways to liven up your walks, as you explore your surroundings and learn about the amazing world around you. Climb trees, roll down hills, gaze at clouds and watch sunsets. Build dens, fly homemade kites, set trails and shadow hop. Hunt for fossils, skim rocks, look for mythical creatures and make music. Splash, create, collect, measure, look, listen, identify, admire... and much more.

As you have probably already realised, there's more to a walk than just walking!

What's so good about walking? ☺

- ✓ Fresh air and exercise make us feel happy
- ✓ It's nice to spend time with family and friends
- ✓ Exercise is good for a healthy heart
- ✓ Our muscles and bones get stronger
- ✓ We get vitamins from sunlight
- ✓ Walking leaves us feeling energised
- ✓ Exercise helps us focus and concentrate
- ✓ We become more aware of nature and our environment
- ✓ There are so many places to explore!

Before you head off

If you're only heading out for a quick stroll, you won't need much at all. But for a longer walk, it's worth taking a rucksack and packing it with the following items:

- Waterproof jacket
- Plenty of water
- Snacks
- Mobile phone and battery charger
- Map
- First aid kit (e.g. plasters, insect cream, painkillers, anti-allergy tablets)
- Tissues
- Antibacterial gel
- Sunscreen and sun hat, if it's warm
- Cosy hat, gloves and an extra pair of socks, if it's chilly

THINK AHEAD
Plan a route before you leave, and always check the weather forecast!

Make sure you are dressed for the weather conditions. Layers are best, so you can add or remove them as the temperature changes.

Some of the crafts in this book require simple materials from home. Check the 'You will need' list before you head out.

Respect the great outdoors

Being out in the open – whether walking in rolling countryside, through shady woodlands, up rocky mountains, along windswept beaches or busy city streets – can give you an amazing sense of freedom. But there are some basic rules you should be aware of. Follow these to ensure the great outdoors remains great, so that other people can enjoy it too – both now and in the future.

- Get to know signs and symbols, and stick to tracks and footpaths.

- Never walk on, or damage, other people's property.

- Don't climb over walls, cut through hedges etc, unless they are signposted.

- Leave gates as you find them, or follow the instructions on signs.

- Be considerate to those living and working in the area you are walking.

- Take care not to damage plants or other natural features.

- Never approach livestock or other wild animals.

- If you have a dog with you, keep it on a lead around livestock and busy roads – and always bag and bin its poo!

- Be considerate of other walkers – walk in single file wherever a path gets narrow, or stand to one side you have to.

- Be nice and say a friendly hello to other walkers, especially if you are resting (so they know you don't need help!).

- Do not light fires and only have BBQs where signs say you can.

- Take your litter home with you.

Stay safe

It's always important to put safety first, so you can relax and make memories without any worries.

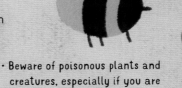

- Always walk with a responsible grown-up – never go off on your own or with friends.

- If you're heading out on a long hike in a rural location, it's a good idea to let someone else know where your group is going, especially as mobile phone signals can be unreliable.

- When walking on roads, always face oncoming traffic so you can move out of the way if needed.

- Beware of poisonous plants and creatures, especially if you are in an area that's known for them.

- Take extra care around water, and be aware of tide times if you are walking near beaches or coastal rivers.

- Be sure to always read signs and never go anywhere that might be dangerous!

Now you know the basics, read on to discover lots of different ideas to pump up the excitement on your walks. Head out, explore and have fun – wherever you end up going!

Explore and discover

Grab your walking boots and let the adventure begin! Whether you're heading out straight after breakfast, taking a leisurely afternoon stroll, or grabbing a torch and hiking after dark, there's so much to learn about your surroundings. Keep your eyes and ears peeled and take it all in.

Let's go!

1 Learn to read a map

First, let's master the basics. The ability to read a map isn't necessary for every walk you'll go on, but it's a really useful skill and will certainly come in handy at some point in your life.

A map is essentially a picture of an area from above. It has symbols to show what and where things are, and different coloured lines to represent roads, rivers, pathways and boundaries. Most maps have a key to show what all the symbols and coloured lines mean.

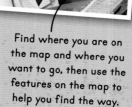

Find where you are on the map and where you want to go, then use the features on the map to help you find the way.

Some maps use contour lines to show the height of the land. Everything along a line is at roughly the same height.

Contour lines arranged inside each other in a loose circular shape show a hill – the closer together the lines, the steeper the slope.

2 Use a compass

A compass is a tool for showing directions, such as north, south, east and west. It has a magnetic needle that always points north – and once you know which way is north, you can work out all the other directions too.

Being able to use a compass is an especially useful skill if you walk in rural locations with few landmarks to guide you.

Make a leaf compass

Pack a needle and magnet and make your own compass!

You will need:

★ A magnet
★ A sewing needle
★ A flat leaf
★ A puddle or bowl of water

1. Rub the magnet along the needle lots of times in the same direction to magnetise it. Ask a grown-up to help.

2. Float the leaf on the water.

3. Carefully place the magnetised needle on top of the leaf.

4. The needle and the leaf will rotate to point north!

③ Plan an interesting route

Preparation is everything! With the help of a map, plan a journey that includes things you'd like to see or do. Ask a grown-up for help searching online for a recommended walking route, or buy a guide book to inspire you. It's usually best to start your walk at (or near) a car park or public transport stop, and it's always a good idea to factor in a toilet break if it's likely to take more than an hour or two!

You could choose to include landmarks you'd like to visit, natural elements such as streams and waterfalls, or simply a breathtaking view!

④ Discover history

History is all around us. Sometimes you need to know where to look, but often it's in full view. Research your destination before you head off, then keep an eye out for clues.

Visit a place of historical interest on your walk, such as a castle, a village with lots of old buildings, or an area with caves and ancient paintings. Look for place names that might suggest the types of people who lived in the area or what used to be there. Some places are named after famous people or events – can you figure out how they are connected to the area?

Make links with people and places from the past. Try to imagine what everything looked like all those years ago, how people lived and what they wore. How is life different today?

⑤ Keep a walking journal

Record your trekking adventures in your own special book. Jot down details such as where you went and how far you travelled, then add drawings or photos. You could buy a ready-made walking journal to fill in, or make your own by decorating and personalising a blank notebook.

Allow time during your walk to sit and make some notes, or fill the book in when you get home. Remember to include the date and time, the location, who you were with and what the weather was like. You could even give the walk a funny title and a mark out of ten!

What to include...

★ How long was the walk?
★ Who were you with?
★ What was the weather like?
★ Did you spot any wildlife?
★ How did the walk make you feel?
★ Would you like to do the walk again?

Create a key to record your information.

Pack a kit so you can fill in your journal while you're out and about. Include pens, pencils, paints, sticky tape and an envelope to collect interesting bits of nature, tickets or leaflets.

14

⑥ Get measuring

That stick you just tripped over might be MASSIVE, but how long is it exactly? What about the teeny leaf that just floated down in front of you – is it smaller than the little fluffy feather you found on your last walk? Take a ruler or tape measure with you and record some stats! Jot down your findings in your journal, so you can compare measurements taken on different walks.

Try estimating before you measure. How near was your guess? Did anyone in your group get closer?

If you have a favourite route you regularly visit, measure the same things each time to see if and how they change size through the seasons.

Why stop at measuring length? Take a tape measure to record the circumference of a tree trunk, or even use some kitchen scales to see how much things weigh!

Note measurements you see when out and about. Some rivers have markers showing how high the water can get. This one is on the River Ouse in England.

7 Look closely

Get up close to nature and gain a whole new viewpoint on what's around you. Pack a magnifying glass to help you get a better look, and get down on your hands and knees to discover things you wouldn't usually see as you're walking along.

Look at plants, rocks and tree bark and see what you can find. Just be careful what you touch if you're in an area known for nasty bugs!

What to look for...

★ Different shades of colour on the petals of a flower

★ The bumpy veins on the underside of a leaf

★ An upside-down reflection in a raindrop

★ The different shapes that make up grains of sand

Use a phone or camera to take lots of close-up photos and challenge your group to identify what they see!

8 Spot patterns in nature

Patterns are all around us. It's easy to see the human-made ones, such as painted lines on a road or the arrangement of bricks in a wall, but nature is full of patterns too. We don't always notice them, but they are there!

You could try looking for simple spots and stripes, or you could see if you can find more mathematical patterns such as spiralling, symmetry and branching – all of which can be found in nature. How many different types of pattern can you find?

Be warned – once you start spotting patterns, it's hard to stop!

Ferns are a perfect example of a fractal. This is when a pattern is repeated across different scales.

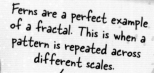

9 Take on a teeny-tiny challenge

Using a small container, such as a matchbox, a small gift box or a plastic tub, collect as many different natural things as you can. At the end of your walk, carefully empty your container and award yourself a point for each item.

Compete against a fellow walker (you must have the same size box!), or try and beat your previous high score each time you go out.

Can you name everything for a bonus point?

Rules
1. Only collect natural objects.
2. You must be able to fit the lid on.
3. No living creatures allowed.
4. All items must be different – repeats are for cheats!

Here are some ideas to get you started...

A piece of bark

A little twig

A tiny leaf

A small pebble

A downy feather

10 Collect and dissect

You might know what a daisy looks like from the outside, but what's inside its yellow middle? And have you ever wondered what a sycamore seed looks like cut in half? Spend time on your walk collecting bits and pieces to dissect (take apart) with the help of a grown-up when you get home.
Do some research online about the items you have collected and discover what all their different parts are called.

REMEMBER: If you're picking flowers, only pick wildflowers that you are certain are not endangered and are safe to handle. And NEVER EVER collect living creatures to dissect at home, that's not good!

Do you know why flowers are brightly coloured? It's to attract pollinators – insects that help them reproduce – such as bees and butterflies.

11 Build a den

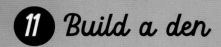

How do you fancy having your own special base in the woods? It could be somewhere to shelter from the elements, eat your lunch or spot birds and other wildlife from. Gather as many large, fallen sticks and branches as you can manage and follow these instructions to create a cosy space for you and your walking companions.

How to make a teepee–style woodland den

1. Find a strong tree with a low fork in the trunk.

2. Gather long, straight sticks and branches from the ground and lean a few of them in the fork, spaced apart, to make a frame for your den.

3. Add more long sticks to fill the spaces. Your den doesn't have to look neat, but it does need to be sturdy. Remember to leave a space for the entrance.

4. If you like, you can fill in the small gaps between the branches with little sticks, bracken and moss, and cover the floor with a carpet of fallen leaves.

LOOK AFTER NATURE
Don't break off branches or damage trees. Only use what you can find on the ground.

You could also make a den by resting branches against a fallen tree. Just make sure it's super-safe beforehand!

TAKE CARE!
Watch out for dangerous creepy crawlies lurking under logs and fallen branches if they're likely to live in your area!

TOP TIP!
Avoid boggy or sloped ground when choosing your den location.

Make a mini den
If you're struggling to find plenty of large branches, make a teeny-tiny den with smaller sticks for teddies and toys to hang out in – or even fairies!

Once you've finished using your den, dismantle it. If you've used any unnatural materials, such as string, rope or fabric, make sure you take them home.

19

12 Wildlife watch

Use a woodland den as a secret hide to observe wildlife, or find a quiet location in a park or near the beach and see what you can spot. Set yourself a time limit (around 20 minutes is good, but just do what you can) and jot down the names of all the creatures you see. Look closely at the ground, into the distance, up to the sky – you could even make a note of any pets!

Record your findings in a journal or on a piece of paper. Create a tally chart if you spot lots of the same animal, and create an extra column for creatures you can hear rather than see.

Sit as still as you can and keep quiet. Animals are likely to be startled by talking or sudden movements!

Try doing a wildlife watch at dawn or dusk. Do you spot different birds and animals at these times of the day?

If you're struggling to identify a creature, take a photo and do some research when you get home.

13 Listen for the birdie

Whether you are walking in the countryside, along the coast or through a city park, you are pretty much guaranteed to hear some kind of birdsong or call. Spring is a good time to listen out for birds singing and communicating with each other, but the calls can be difficult to identify at first.

Before you head out, find a website or app that has birdsong samples and familiarise yourself with some of the most common ones, or use a smartphone while you're out on your walk to help you.

Pick a spot to sit really quietly and tune in. Somewhere near trees or bushes is ideal, and if you are able to go out at dawn or dusk you'll hear even more. Listen carefully, then see if you can figure out where a sound is coming from to help you identify the bird by sight.

TOP TIP
Stumped by what you hear? Record the birdsong on a smartphone and do more research when you get home.

If you keep a walking journal, log your findings. What words would you use to communicate the types of sounds you hear?

Words to help you describe what you hear...

rapid

repetitive

relaxed

shrill

clear

LOUD

high-pitched

URGENT

mellow

lively

low

14 Become an animal detective

You don't need any special qualifications to become this kind of detective, just curiosity and excellent observational skills! Hunt for clues, piece them together and discover which furry or feathered friends visited your location before you.

Searching for evidence of wildlife is called animal tracking, and it can be done at any time of year. Looking for footprints in soft ground or snow is one of the simplest ways to track animals, but it isn't the only way. You can look for tufts of fur caught on fences, feathers on the ground, scratches on tree trunks – even piles of poo!

Look carefully for owl pellets. These contain the parts of an owl's prey that it cannot digest, such as bones, beaks and teeth. Pellets are cast (spat) back up out of an owl's mouth.

Early civilisations would use animal tracking skills to hunt for food. For some indigenous peoples, it is still part of everyday life.

TAKE CARE

Never get close to a wild animal, even if it appears friendly.

An apple that has a hole in its side and much of its flesh eaten may have been a bird's dinner.

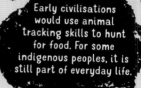

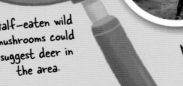

Half–eaten wild mushrooms could suggest deer in the area.

Horse hoof prints on the old farm track!

Which animal created these scratches?

We spotted some deer tracks near the forest.

I wonder which bird this feather belonged to?

Animal fur! What could it be from?

Rabbit droppings near the canal!

HANDS OFF!
Don't ever touch poo! It may contain harmful bacteria.

Dung deciphering

To help you work out whose poo is whose...

★ Look at its shape, size and colour.

★ Break it apart with a stick to see what the animal has eaten - there may be clues within!

★ Use an app to help you.

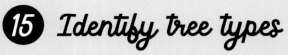

15 Identify tree types

Do you know your birch tree from your beech tree? Or your walnut from your willow? No? Fear not – there are plenty of apps, online printables and identification guidebooks available to help you become an expert in no time at all!

All trees fall into one of two types, deciduous or evergreen. The main difference is that deciduous trees lose their leaves in autumn and grow new leaves in spring, while evergreen trees keep their leaves all year round.

Download an app to help you work out what different trees are called. Some can cleverly identify the tree from a photo of a leaf. Other apps ask you questions about the tree – about its shape, colour, bark pattern, blossom, seeds and fruit – and will identify the tree from the answers you give!

Deciduous tree

Evergreen tree

Use your other senses to help identify trees too. What does the bark feel like? Does the tree smell? Do the leaves rustle in the breeze?

24

16 Shake a tree

Gently shake a tree to find out what lives in it. Technically it's called 'tree beating' but it's not as violent as it sounds; trees and bugs aren't hurt! Take an old tea towel or pillowcase on your walk, lay it on the ground and shake away. Watch out for falling fruit in autumn!

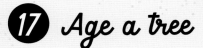

White fabric works best, as it shows everything clearly.

This tree would have been about 40 years old when it was cut down.

17 Age a tree

It's no myth that you can work out the age a tree was when it was cut down by counting its rings. Trees grow fastest in the spring and summer, so the wood produced behind the bark during this time is lighter. Over autumn and winter trees grow much more slowly, producing a darker wood. Counting the number of dark rings from the centre of the stump outwards will tell you how many cold seasons the tree lived through, which is the same as the number of years it was alive.

STOP!

Of course, don't cut down a tree just to find out how old it is! There are other ways to work out a tree's age, such as measuring around the trunk with a tape measure. If you know what type of tree you are measuring you can use an online tree aging calculator to work out how old it is likely to be.

25

⑱ Explore a watery world

Grab your wellies so you can make a lake, stream, river or beach part of your walking route.

Always return creatures to their homes once you've looked at them, ideally within a few minutes.

Pond-dipping

Ponds and lakes are teeming with unseen wildlife beneath the surface of the water, especially in the summer months. Scoop a jam jar, bucket, sieve or fishing net through the water and study your findings. It's really useful to have an app or identification sheet to help you understand what's what, so download or print one out before you go.

Rock-pooling

If you're near the coast, go rock-pooling and get friendly with saltwater creatures instead. Check tide times online, then head to the beach about an hour before low tide to get plenty of animal-spotting time.

Make a splash!

A summer's day, a shallow, gently-flowing stream and an hour or so of free time are the perfect ingredients for adding a bit of fun into your walk. Simply take off your shoes, paddle, splash and enjoy!

SAFETY FIRST

★ Be extra careful near water, and only explore shallow, calm areas.

★ Make sure you have a grown-up with you.

★ Be sure to cover any cuts or open wounds with waterproof plasters before playing in rivers or lakes.

★ Always wash your hands afterwards.

★ Don't drink the water!

For more water activities, check out how to skim stones on page 53 and the raft-building instructions on pages 80–81.

It's always a good idea to pack spare clothes if you're exploring in and around water, just in case!

19 Spot animal homes

All wildlife needs a place to live, just like us humans, but animals can only live in areas they are adapted to. This is called their habitat.

What kind of habitat is the area you are walking in? What types of creatures might live there? Can you see any of their homes? Some are easy to spot, like spider webs, bird nests and beehives, but there are less obvious ones too, such as hollowed-out tree trunks, burrows and holes. It can be quite tricky to identify the occupants of some of these homes, so you might need the help of an app, website or guidebook!

BE A FRIEND TO NATURE

Never touch or disturb an animal's home.

Many animals dig and burrow into the ground to make their homes, such as foxes, rabbits and ants.

A fox den in a tree hollow

If you come across any creatures while exploring, either keep very still or back away slowly so as not to frighten them.

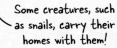

Some creatures, such as snails, carry their homes with them!

20 Identify clouds

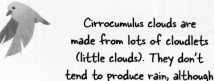

It's always a good idea to check the weather forecast before you head out. But if you don't manage to, then pay attention to the sky instead. The colour of the sky – and clouds in particular – can tell us a lot about the current weather conditions. They can even let us see into the future, as we can use them to predict what the weather will do next!

Clouds are made up of millions of tiny water droplets or ice crystals which have evaporated into the air from Earth's surface. Each type of cloud has a different name, and can be identified by its shape, size, pattern and position in the sky.

There are three main groups of clouds: cirrus, cumulus and stratus. Cirrus clouds are wispy and found high up in the sky, cumulus clouds are puffy and look a bit like cotton-wool, and stratus clouds are flat like a blanket.

Cirrocumulus clouds are made from lots of cloudlets (little clouds). They don't tend to produce rain, although storms can follow.

Cirrocumulus

If the sky is full of nimbostratus clouds, the chances are you are already getting wet. These heavy, grey blankets are full of rain!

Nimbostratus

Cumulus

Cumulus clouds are a sign of fair weather, but on hot days they can quickly turn into cumulonimbus thunderclouds!

Low stratus clouds often bring drizzle, mist or fog.

Stratus

Stratocumulus clouds usually form when stratus clouds start to break up, indicating a change in the weather.

Stratocumulus

Cirrus

High up in the sky, wispy cirrus clouds are usually associated with fair weather.

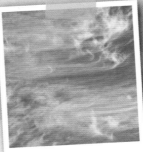

Cirrostratus

Cirrostratus clouds are a thin layer of cloud that you can still see the Sun or Moon through. They often signal rain in the next 12–24 hours.

Altostratus and altocumulus clouds tend to gather a few hours before the weather turns stormy.

Altostratus

Altocumulus

Cumulonimbus

Tall with flat tops, cumulonimbus clouds are easy to recognise. They are responsible for stormy weather, creating hail, thunder and lightning.

BE PREPARED

The faster the clouds are moving, the quicker the weather will change!

WHAT'S IN A NAME?

Cloud names come from Latin. If you can remember the meaning of the following Latin words, you'll get a good idea about a cloud's character, or how high it can be found in the sky.

Cirro (cirrus): curly or wispy, like a lock of hair
Alto: medium level or in the middle
Strato (stratus): flat or layered
Cumulo (cumulus): puffy, heaped or piled
Nimbo (nimbus): rain cloud

21 Become a geologist

Rocks are everywhere! It's pretty much impossible to go on a walk and not see some kind of rock, whether in its natural setting or as a material used to create something.

There are three different types of rock – igneous, sedimentary and metamorphic.

TYPES OF ROCK

★ Igneous rocks are volcanic and are formed when lava or magma cools and hardens.

★ Sedimentary rocks are made up of lots of fragments of rocks, minerals or plant remains which have gathered and been squashed together over a very long time.

★ Metamorphic rock is a type of rock that has been changed by extreme heat or pressure.

At the beach

Coastal areas are especially fantastic for rock-spotting, particularly if there are cliffs nearby or a pebbly beach. Look for layers of rock in cliff faces, and see for yourself how erosion and the movement of land over time has created different patterns. Take a closer look at pebbles on the beach – can you see streaks of quartz or other minerals running through them? Feel how smooth and rounded they have become by being tossed around in the waves.

Use a rock identification app to help you work out which type of rocks you see on your walk, and make a note of your findings in a journal.

HOW ARE ROCKS MADE?

Rocks are created by minerals growing or fusing together. All rocks are made from one or more minerals.

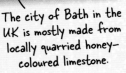

Historically, buildings would have been made from whatever stone was commonly found in an area. You can still see evidence of this today.

The city of Bath in the UK is mostly made from locally quarried honey-coloured limestone.

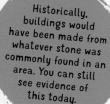

Coastal erosion due to weather and waves can result in unique rock formations.

Layers of sedimentary rock can sometimes be seen on inland cliffs.

22 Go on a fossil hunt

Fossils are the preserved remains or traces of dead animals or plants that lived a very long time ago. They are formed when layers of earth and sediment pile on top and harden into rock, preserving the fossil beneath it. Hard bones, shells and teeth can leave imprints in the rock that has hardened around them. These imprints are a type of fossil, too!

You can find fossils in many places, but coastal areas are often the best fossil-hunting destinations. Here, waves crash into the shore, eating away rocks and revealing fossils for all to see. If you're nowhere near the coast, research online with a grown-up to see whether there are any areas local to you, possibly near rivers or rocky outcrops, where fossils have been found.

Fossil ammonite in Dorset, England

Fossil-hunting helps us connect the past to the present, but you do need some patience and perseverance.

Keep away from cliff faces when exploring as loose rocks can fall.

Ammonite fossils are often found in coastal areas. These prehistoric shelled sea creatures ranged in size from under 1 cm (0.5 in) to around 1.8 m (6 ft) in diameter!

A good time to go fossil-hunting on a beach is after a storm. Just make sure the weather has calmed down before you visit!

If you find a fossil, check whether you are allowed to take it home. If you're not sure, it's best to just leave it for others to enjoy.

23 Watch the Sun set

See the evening skies come ablaze with fiery colour! While sunsets occur every evening, to get the most out of your experience, it's best to do a bit of planning. Check online to find out what time the Sun will set in your part of the world, and get into position at least half an hour in advance to see the full show.

GONE ALREADY!

It takes around 8 minutes for light from the Sun to reach us on Earth. So sunset actually occurs around 8 minutes before we see it happening!

If you can, watch the Sun set over a body of water, such as the sea or a lake. You will get an awesome reflection!

HOW DOES THE SUN SET?

The Sun doesn't actually 'set' – it stays in the same position at the centre of our Solar System all the time. Earth, however, rotates as it travels through space, so the Sun appears to move down in the sky as your location on Earth turns away from it.

SUNSET TIPS

★ Go on a clear evening, with little or no cloud.

★ Find a spot with a clear view to the west.

★ Don't look directly at the Sun, but instead look at all the wonderful colours in the sky.

★ Once the Sun has set, it will start to feel chilly, even if it has been a hot day, so take a blanket and some warm layers.

24 Go on a bat hunt

If you're out walking at dusk on a balmy evening, keep your eyes peeled for bats as they leave their roosts and dive through the air to catch insects. Bats hibernate in winter and they don't like rain, so a warm, dry, summer's evening is the best time to spot them looping and swooping. You're best off looking for them near water and at the edge of woods because these areas have plenty of tiny flying insects, although bats can also be spotted in built-up areas too.

Find out whether there are any organised bat walks in your local area that you can join.

25 Torch walk

Going for a walk at night can be really exciting, as you can't rely on your sense of sight as much. Take a torch, a flask of warm milk or hot chocolate and a grown-up – and don't forget to wrap up warm!

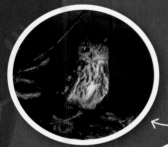

Some animals are nocturnal, which means they only come out at night. Can you spot any?

TRY THESE ACTIVITIES

★ Shine your torch on trees to make spooky shadows.

★ Change the colour of your torch beam by fixing coloured see-through sweet wrappers over the lens.

★ Stop somewhere safe and switch off the torch, letting your eyes become accustomed to the night.

★ Think of some spooky stories to entertain (and scare!) your fellow walkers.

★ Listen out for animal sounds. Can you hear different sounds at night from those you hear in the day?

Pick a moonlit night and you won't need to use a torch all the time. Instead, you can use light from the Moon to show you the way.

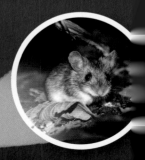

33

26 Go stargazing

You don't need any special equipment for stargazing – just head out on a clear night and look up!

For thousands of years, humans have looked to the stars to guide them, using the sky as a giant map. During the day, sailors and other travellers would use the Sun's position to help them work out which way to go. After dark, they would be guided by the position of the stars.

Throughout the night, and at different times of the year, the stars appear to change position, moving across the sky. This is because Earth rotates on its axis and around the Sun, so our viewpoint varies. However, the stars always remain in the same location relative to one another.

Where do you live?

The night sky looks different depending on whether you are in the Northern or Southern Hemisphere.

NORTHERN HEMISPHERE

If you're in the Northern Hemisphere, a star called Polaris (also known as the North Star) will show you which direction is north. The North Star always stays above the Earth's North Pole.

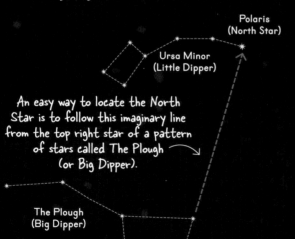

Polaris
(North Star)

Ursa Minor
(Little Dipper)

An easy way to locate the North Star is to follow this imaginary line from the top right star of a pattern of stars called The Plough (or Big Dipper).

The Plough
(Big Dipper)

SOUTHERN HEMISPHERE

If you're in the Southern Hemisphere, you can tell which way is south by locating the Southern Cross constellation.

Southern
Cross

The arrow shows which direction is south.

For the best stargazing experience:

★ Choose a clear night with no cloud.
★ Take a blanket to lie on.
★ Wear warm clothes.
★ Find somewhere away from the glare of town and city street lights.
★ Allow time for your eyes to become used to the dark, then you will see more.
★ Make sure you have company – don't go out at night without a grown-up's permission.

There are plenty of resources available to help you identify what you see. Look for printable downloads of monthly star charts for your part of the world, or use the NASA app which allows you to point a phone at the night sky and identify the stars and planets. You could also take a look at Lonely Planet Kids' *Amazing Night Sky Atlas* to learn more on this fascinating subject.

27 Study the Moon's phases

The phases of the Moon are what we call the amount of Moon that can be seen from Earth over the space of a month. As the Sun lights up different parts of the Moon, it appears to grow from a thin sliver (crescent) to a complete circle (full Moon), then shrink to a crescent Moon again before disappearing altogether for a couple of nights (this is called a new Moon).

The next time you head out after dark, take a look at the Moon. What type of Moon can you see?

Waxing crescent

First quarter (half Moon)

Full Moon

Third quarter (half Moon)

Waning crescent

When the Moon appears to be growing, it is called 'waxing'. The opposite is 'waning'.

The Moon doesn't create its own light. When we see the Moon shining, what we are actually seeing is sunlight reflecting off it.

35

Activities and things to do

Now you've learnt all about your surroundings, add excitement by setting yourself and your walking buddies some fun challenges. Make an obstacle course, lay tracks, play with shadows or fly a kite. Alternatively, slow down and try a spot of meditation or yoga. No two walks need to be the same – find something different to do each time you head out!

28 Hike up a hill

Reward yourself with some amazing views and an awesome sense of achievement by climbing a hill – or even a mountain! Walking up hills and mountains can be hard work, but extremely satisfying. Once you reach the peak you'll feel on top of the world!

This is something you'll need to do with a grown-up. You could also ask them to help you do some research. Find out the best place to start, and have a route planned-out in advance. Check distances and work out roughly how long the climb will take.

Be sure to look at the weather forecast before you set off. The best conditions for hill-climbing are dry and sunny or with light cloud, but not too hot, too cold or windy.

Top tips

★ Set out early to allow yourself plenty of time.

★ Take lots of drinks and snacks – you'll need them for energy. No-one wants a hungry, grumpy walking companion!

★ Be sure someone in the group has a fully charged mobile phone, along with a printed map for back-up in case the phone battery runs dead.

★ Dress properly! Walking boots and plenty of layers will allow you to adapt what you're wearing to the weather conditions, and a waterproof will come in handy if the weather turns.

BIG HILL OR MOUNTAIN?

Believe it or not, there is no official difference between a hill and a mountain, although it's generally agreed that mountains are taller than hills. Mountains are also considered to have a pointier peak, steeper faces (sides) and they usually belong to a named mountain range.

29 Roll down a grassy slope

If you've never laid on your side at the top of a grassy mound and let yourself roll down it, you don't know what you're missing! It's one of the simplest, most fun things to do on a walk – just check there are no dangers such as rocks, bushes, posts or holes before you launch your body downhill!

Can you convince a grown-up to join in too? It's likely to be more fun than they expect!

There are all sorts of reasons why rolling down a hill is good for you.

★ It wakes up your muscles and ligaments.

★ It challenges your balance (which is why you feel giddy afterwards).

★ It makes you giggle, and that releases endorphins (feel-good chemicals) which make you feel happier.

30 Let a coin decide the way

If you don't mind where you end up, whenever you get to a fork in the path or a junction, toss a coin and let it decide the route. Heads for left, tails for right – or devise your own rules. Just make sure someone is making a note of how to get back again!

39

(31) Admire the scenery

Give your walk the wow factor by finding a route with a spectacular view. You don't have to climb to the very top of a mountain – depending on where you are, smaller hills, buildings, bridges and other human-made structures can also provide you with an amazing vantage point.

What to look for...

★ Look to the horizon, or the furthest thing you can see. How far away do you think it is?

★ Turn around slowly through 360° and see whether you can work out which way is north, south, east and west.

★ Do you see any landmarks and are you able to name them? Use a map to help you.

★ Can you spot places you have previously visited? Where have you come from, and in which direction are you heading?

★ Pick out a building or unusual feature. What do you think it is used for? Will people be there right now? What could they be doing? Do you think they can see you?

CAPTURE IT!

Pack a sketchbook and some pens, pencils or watercolour paints, then sketch what you can see from high up.

Create a panoramic view by taking several photos from the same position. Print them out when you get home, then create a montage.

LOG IT

Stick printed photos and sketches into a journal (see page 14) and build up a collection of your favourite views!

SPOTTING FUN

While you have so much to look at, it's the perfect opportunity for a mega-session of 'I spy'. Check out page 88 for different ways to play the game.

32 Climb a tree

Visit woodland or a forest on a dry day and you'll find yourself in the middle of a huge natural playground, with growing, living climbing frames of all shapes and sizes to enjoy.

First, look for a strong tree with a thick trunk. Check it has sturdy branches starting fairly close to the ground, then carefully pull yourself up. Reach for branches that you can get to easily without putting yourself off-balance. As you climb, always keep three parts of your body touching the tree (two feet and one hand, or two hands and one foot) and make sure your grip and footing is secure before you make your next move.

Top tree-climbing tips

★ Wet trees are slippery and no fun at all, so make sure the tree you choose is nice and dry.

★ Check for signs of rot before you start - and for wildlife. If you spot any nests, bugs or swarms of bees, move on to another tree.

★ Only climb onto branches thicker than your own leg.

★ Cold temperatures can make wood brittle, so in winter test each branch well before putting your weight on it.

★ Wear sturdy footwear - trainers or walking boots are best.

★ Never attempt to climb a tree in strong wind or a thunderstorm, and avoid trees near power cables.

★ Don't go any higher than you are comfortable with!

Make sure you have a grown-up nearby.

Not all trees are there to be climbed! Some are protected, and not all areas allow it, so check that it's OK first.

Only go up if you are confident you can get back down safely!

33 Hug a tree

As strange as it sounds, hugging a tree can actually improve your mood. Being close to nature can release chemicals called endorphins into your blood stream, which make you feel calmer and happier. We'll probably never know, but the trees might like it too!

Show a tree some love

1. Find a tree with a wide trunk.
2. Stretch your arms around it, spread out your fingers and rest your cheek on its bark.
3. Close your eyes and take a deep breath. Feel the tree's strength and how firmly rooted it is to the ground. If you like, you could even talk to it!

TREE-MENDOUS TREES
Without trees, we wouldn't be alive. They soak up nasty gases from the atmosphere that contribute to climate change, and provide us with oxygen so we can breathe. So think of hugging a tree as a way of saying 'thank you' for giving us life!

34 Make a tree swing

A sturdy tree with a strong horizontal branch and a thick piece of rope is all you need for this activity. Just make sure you've checked that the branch is strong enough to hold your weight first!

You will need to learn how to tie a bowline knot to attach the rope to the branch. Look online or print a guide to help you before you set out. Once you have your bowline knot in place, tie another knot at the dangling end to sit on. Hey presto – you have a swing!

Use a bowline knot to tie the rope to the branch.

Add extra knots along the length to grip on to.

Make sure the swinging area is clear of obstacles and that there are no steep drops or water that you could fall into if you slip off.

35 Create an obstacle course

Who can walk along a fallen branch the quickest? Or leap over the most rocks? Use your surroundings to create an obstacle course for yourself and your fellow walkers, then take it in turns to complete the challenge. Who will be crowned champion?

First, plan your course. Look at everything around you and use as many things that are already in place as possible. Then get creative! Sketch a map with a route to follow, or simply talk it through with your competitors. Once you have all agreed on the rules, take it in turns to tackle the course against the clock.

Here are some suggestions to get you started...

Weave your way in and out of trees.

Run to a pile of logs and back again.

Walk along a log or raised beam.

Climb onto a low branch.

Leap from tree stump to tree stump.

Ideas for other environments...

Avoid cracks in the pavement, skip up steps and swing around lamp posts if your walk takes you through a town or city.

Draw a course in the sand if you're at the beach, or run in and out of pebbles laid in a line.

If you visit a playground, you have a ready-made obstacle course! You just need to think of a route and what to do on each piece of equipment.

44

36 Geocaching

Geocaching (pronounced *jee-oh-cash-ing*) is a bit like an outdoor treasure hunt, using GPS on a mobile phone to guide you as you track special containers known as 'geocaches'. Geocaches can be found all over the world: in towns and cities, at country parks and playgrounds, along bike trails, on piers, up mountains – they could be anywhere! There could be caches hidden in an area you often visit that you have no idea are there!

All you need to go geocaching is a mobile phone. Ask a grown-up to download the Geocaching app and set up a free account before you head out. Then use the app to navigate you to where a geocache is hidden.

Because geocaches are hidden from public view, hunting for one is a bit like being in a secret club. Be discreet when looking, and make sure you hide it well again afterwards, in the exact same place you found it.

SMALL, MEDIUM OR LARGE
Geocaches come in different sizes. The smallest are around the size of a matchbox and just include a tiny logbook to fill in. Bigger caches usually have a logbook along with little toys and trinkets to swap.

Fill in the logbook before re-hiding the cache.

45

③⑦ Learn the art of trailblazing

Also known as tracking or waymarking, trailblazing is the technique of creating a series of marks for other people to follow. In a similar way to how Hansel and Gretel laid a trail of breadcrumbs so they could find their way home, markings are left to show a route – although, as Hansel and Gretel found out, making the trail from something edible isn't the best idea!

This activity is best done as group so you can divide into teams, making sure no one is on their own. You'll need at least four people: two to walk ahead and leave signs, and the others to follow.

AGREE ON YOUR SYMBOLS

Think about what signs you could use and make sure everyone in the group knows their meanings. They could be simple arrows, or something more cryptic!

You could tie coloured strips of wool or ribbon around tree branches or fence posts to mean different things. Make sure the team following removes them.

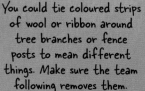

Here are some ideas to start you off, based on traditional tracking symbols...

Straight on

Turn left

Turn right

Wrong way

Caution

The end

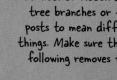

46

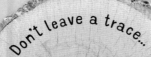

Don't leave a trace...

Be kind to your environment and create signs from nature.

★ Lay sticks to create arrows.

★ Arrange stones in the shape of your symbols.

★ Draw marks with chalk.

★ Scratch signs in soft ground.

Many walking routes are marked with official signs, like this one in the Pyrenees mountains in Europe.

KEEP YOUR EYES OPEN!

When following a trail, keep your eyes peeled at all times. You don't want to miss a symbol!

Trailblaze like a pro

★ Setting up the trail takes longer than following it, so allow plenty of time for the first group to get well underway before the second group sets off.

★ Think about the weather. If it's windy, making symbols out of small twigs and leaves probably won't work.

★ Never create permanent marks or damage property or nature.

★ Have a backup plan in case the trail gets destroyed or anyone gets lost. A grown-up in the group following could be trusted to keep the destination secret, or the groups could contact each other by phone. Or simply agree to meet back at the start if things go wrong!

38 Count your steps

Does someone in your group have a fitness tracker or step counter? Play a game of 'guess the steps' – agree on a landmark up ahead and estimate how many steps it will take to get there. The closest wins! Or do the guessing at the end of your walk. Who completed the most steps and who did the least? (Hint – the answers are most likely to be related to leg length!)

3564

Keep a tally of steps walked in your journal (see page 14). Could you set yourself a target of achieving a certain number of steps in a month, and raise money for charity by getting sponsored to complete the challenge?

If you're feeling keen, rather than counting steps you could count in kilometres!

39 Stop and shop

Rest your feet and support a local business at the same time. Independent cafés, coffee shops, ice-cream sellers, food trucks and farm shops rely on getting business from passers-by just like you, and it's the perfect opportunity to refuel and rest your weary legs. Plan a stop-off midway, grab an ice lolly or a hot chocolate and recharge your batteries before continuing your journey.

WHAT'S AN INDEPENDENT SHOP?

Independent shops are often run by just one or two people, or a family, and they usually have just one store.

40 Feed the ducks

If your walk goes near a river, lake or pond, the chances are you'll meet some waterfowl, such as ducks, swans or geese. Come prepared with some carefully chosen food for them, and you'll be their new best friend!

Good food for ducks

★ Oats

★ Seeds

★ Rice – cooked or uncooked

★ Peas and sweetcorn. They don't need to be cooked, but frozen veg does need to be defrosted.

Not-so-good food for ducks

★ Bread. It isn't nutritious and it fills them up, which means they then won't eat the food they should be eating.

★ Chips, biscuits and sweets. They aren't good for us, and they aren't good for ducks either!

TAKE CARE

Always be super-careful around water and stand well back from the water's edge.

Feed in small amounts. If the ducks don't appear hungry, stop feeding them, as excess food can attract disease-carrying rats.

Throw your food into the water rather than on the banks, as ducks are safer from predators there than they are on land.

Don't get too close to wildlife — try and keep a good distance away.

WARNING!

While our feathered friends are more than happy to receive specially selected snacks, the stomachs of horses and other animals you may meet are very sensitive. Don't ever feed them, as they can get extremely sick.

41 Make and fly a kite

Wide, open spaces – such as beaches, fields or country parks – are fantastic locations for kite-flying. You just need a gentle breeze, a bit of patience – and, of course, a kite!

Make your own kite

Don't worry if you don't already own one. You can make a simple kite from a piece of paper, a couple of sticks and some string before you head out.

You will need:
- ★ A3 or A4 paper or thin card
- ★ Two thin sticks, one the same height as the paper, the other the same width as the paper
- ★ Sticky tape
- ★ Scissors
- ★ Pencil
- ★ Thin string, around 7 m (23 ft) long
- ★ One thick stick, about 20 cm (8 in) long

❶ Fold the paper in half lengthways, then unfold. Fold it again, about one third down from the top edge, then unfold. You will now have two creases, as shown.

❷ Lay the thin sticks along the creases, so they cross at right angles, then tape them in place. Cut along the paper from the tip of each stick to make a diamond shape.

❸ With a pencil, carefully poke two small pairs of holes through the paper, either side of the sticks, as shown. Turn the kite over so the sticks are underneath.

❹ Cut two pieces of string the same size as the kite's width. For each string, pass one end through one hole in a pair, around the stick beneath it, and back out the other hole. Then tie a knot near to the kite, leaving one long end of string.

❺ Tie the two long ends of string together to make a secure knot. Take the remaining length of string and tie one end of it to the knot you just made.

❻ Tie the other end of the long piece of string around a thick stick, to make a handle. Wind the string around the handle until you are ready to launch!

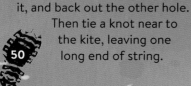

How to fly your kite

You might only need a bit of wind, but getting your kite up in the sky – and keeping it there – can be tricky. Follow these tips and your kite will be flying high in no time!

❶ You'll need another person to hold the kite (the launcher), while you operate the handle and string. Holding the handle and string, stand with your back to the wind, with the launcher facing you.

❷ Unwind the string a few metres as the launcher walks backwards, keeping the string pulled taut.

❸ The launcher lifts the kite until the wind catches it, then pushes it upwards and lets go. If there's enough wind, the kite should continue to lift up until it is fully airborne.

❹ Let the string out to make the kite fly higher. The wind is strongest high up in the sky, so once it's up it should be fairly easy to keep the kite there!

TOP TIP
Personalise your kite by adding ribbons made from thin strips of paper or decorating it with felt-tip pens and pencils.

To bring the kite back down to the ground, simply wind in the string.

If your kite starts to dive, push your arm forwards to loosen the tension on the string.

Stay safe

★ Make sure you find a quiet spot with plenty of space.

★ Check there are no trees nearby or dangerous overhead cables.

★ Never fly a kite in a thunderstorm!

42 Eat in the fresh air

Walking uses energy. Lots of it! And all that energy will need replacing, so pack a hearty picnic full of nutritious goodies. Find a peaceful spot to sit and eat midway through your walk. You could make the break extra-special by stopping off somewhere with an awesome view.

Cut picnic waste

★ Avoid individually wrapped items. Instead, pack large bags of snacks to share.

★ Take your own drinks from home, rather than buying drinks in plastic bottles.

★ Pack sandwiches and salad vegetables in washable tubs, or use a beeswax wrap to keep them fresh.

★ Use a dampened cloth or flannel to clean sticky fingers instead of environmentally unfriendly wet wipes.

CLEAR UP

Make sure to take any rubbish home with you and leave your picnicking spot exactly as you found it.

Energy-boosting flapjacks

With a grown-up's help, make these tasty snacks at home before you head out!

- Preheat the oven to 190°C (170°C fan); gas mark 5.
- Line a shallow baking tin with greaseproof paper.
- Mix the fruit, cornflakes, oats and flour together in a large bowl.
- Melt the butter, sugar and syrup together.
- Carefully pour the melted liquid into the dry ingredients and stir well.
- Press the mixture into the baking tin and bake for around 18 minutes.
- Leave to cool, then cut into squares.

Ingredients

★ 85 g (3 oz) butter
★ 85 g (3 oz) light brown sugar
★ 1 tbsp golden syrup or honey
★ 150 g (5 oz) chopped dried fruit – a mixture of sultanas, apricots and glacé cherries works well
★ 85 g (3 oz) crushed cornflakes
★ 60 g (2 oz) oats
★ 60 g (2 oz) self-raising flour

43 Race sticks

If your walk takes you across a bridge that goes over a river or stream, challenge your companions to a stick race. This classic game is a bit daft, but lots of fun! Each person finds a stick. Everyone then throws their stick from one side of the bridge at the same time, in the direction that the water is coming from. Then you all run to the other side of the bridge to see whose stick comes out first. It's that simple!

Try to find sticks that are slightly different, so you can tell them apart as they race.

44 Make a stone bounce

With a bit of practice, you can defy gravity and make a stone skip across water. You just need to find a perfectly shaped stone and learn how to throw it the right way.

THROW LIKE A PRO
It's all in the spin. Once you've mastered this, your stones will be skipping effortlessly across the surface of the water.

❶ Find a large area of still water, such as a lake or calm river.
❷ Choose a thin, flat, round stone that you can hold comfortably in your hand. The best way to hold it is with your index finger curled around the edge and your thumb on top, across the flat area.
❸ Crouch down low and aim towards the water, holding your hand so the stone is horizontal.
❹ While you throw the stone, try to spin it with your index finger. Flicking your wrist will help too.
❺ If you get it right, you'll see the stone bounce across the water, as if by magic!

BE CAREFUL!
Never throw stones in the direction of people or wildlife.

Stone-skimming is actually a sport! Each year, competitors from all over the globe compete at The World Stone Skimming Championships in Scotland.

53

45 Have fun with shadows

On a sunny day, you'll be surrounded by shadows. They're always there, just waiting to be played with – and the best thing is, they won't go away until the Sun sets, or the sky clouds over!

Shadow art

Make interesting shapes, using either your body or items gathered on your walk and create art from the shadows that form. Can you hunch over to create a scary shadow monster, or arrange sticks and stones to create a shady scene from your favourite book or film? Take a photo of your shadow art to capture it before it disappears.

WHAT IS A SHADOW?

Shadows are made when something opaque (not see-through) blocks out the light. A shadow is formed in the opposite direction to the light source.

Use things you find in nature as props or extra elements for your art. For example, empty snail shells and feathers laid on the ground could make good eyes and hair for a shadow monster. Or you could add funny features to faces by drawing in sand or dust.

Take photos with a phone and use editing tools (along with your imagination) to turn shadows into other things.

Shadow puppets

You can also have fun with shadow puppets in the daytime if the Sun is strong enough. Either create characters with your hands or cut out pieces of paper, then make up a story and put on a show.

A rabbit?

Shadow hopping

Can you get from one point to another by only stepping on shadows? Hop, skip and jump through the shade to your destination. You can step on other people's shadows if you need help crossing an open, sunlit area.

TOP TIP

The best time to play with shadows is in the morning or late afternoon. When the Sun is directly overhead, the shadows will be very short, but earlier or later in the day, they will be longer.

Shadow tag

Similar to a normal game of 'tag', but instead of catching another player, the person who is 'It' has to step on their shadow. That player then becomes 'It'.

46 Slow down and use your senses

It might seem like a crazy idea to slow down on your walk – you are trying to get from A to B, after all. But when you take your time and use all your senses to really appreciate what's going on, you will enjoy the journey even more.

Sight

You might think that this sense is already being used, because you need to look where you're going so you don't bump into anything! This is true, but try using your sense of sight even more by having a really good look at all the interesting things around you and not just at the ground in front of your feet.

Give your eyes a workout!

★ What's the furthest thing you can see?

★ Can you see something for each colour of the rainbow?

★ How many different textures can you spot?

★ How fast are the clouds moving?

If you are lucky enough to own a pair of binoculars, take them with you. Use them to magnify faraway objects and bring them up close!

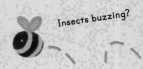

Insects buzzing?

Cars on a nearby road?

The faint drone of an aircraft?

Birdsong?

Sound

Close your eyes and listen. How many different sounds can you hear? Two? Three? Try again. Can you hear any more?

When you listen really carefully you will probably realise that you can hear many individual sounds all at the same time. How many different sounds can you hear?

The wind rustling leaves in the trees?

People chatting or laughing?

A babbling stream?

Smell

We don't usually think about what we can smell on a walk unless it's pretty horrid (er, did someone step in fox poo?!) or something lovely – like freshly baked goodies from a bakery.

Draw up a chart of all the things you can smell on your walk and put them in order from most to least favourite.

Slow down, breathe deeply through your nose and think about the scents around you.

Can you smell any flowers, herbs or trees? How about damp soil, grass or musty moss? If you're near the coast, can you smell the salty sea air, rockpools or sunscreen? Or if you're exploring a more built-up area, how about tarmac being laid or a café brewing coffee?

WHO KNEW?
Our noses can smell and identify millions of different scents! How many can you identify on your walk?

Touch

When we think about touch, we usually think about reaching out and feeling with our fingers. But there's more to it than that!

Can you feel the Sun on your skin? The wind blowing a cool breeze through your hair? Do you have cold toes? Warm hands?

Try going barefoot! Ask your grown-ups if you can take off your socks and shoes and walk barefoot for a while. How does it feel? Soft? Spiky? Uneven? Squidgy?

Taste

We shouldn't eat anything in nature without being 100 per cent certain it's safe. But if you really want to involve your sense of taste on your journey, once you've mastered honing in on all your other senses, find a comfy spot and grab yourself a snack!

47 Meditate

Meditation is a way of relaxing your body and mind, and being surrounded by nature can help give a feeling of even deeper relaxation. Take some time out on your walk to enjoy the benefits that a moment of calm can give you.

First, relax and unwind

Find a place that is quiet and still. Sit yourself down, cross-legged if it's comfortable for you, or lie down on a blanket if you prefer. Take deep breaths, relax and close your eyes...

❶ Focus on what's happening right now. How does your body feel? Tune in to your senses. What can you hear, smell, taste?

❷ What are you thinking about as you breathe in and out? Can you think about your breathing instead?

❸ When you are ready to finish, take in a deep breath of fresh air, wiggle your fingers and toes, and open your eyes.

Meditation techniques

Once you have mastered the basic art of relaxation, you might want to try one of these meditation exercises.

Muscle relaxation

This type of meditation focuses on relaxing different parts of the body one at a time, starting with the head and working down to the toes.

Focus on each part of the body in turn, making sure you relax each muscle group as you go.

Visualisation

Visualisation means imagining what something looks, sounds and smells like, and creating that picture in your mind – a bit like having a dream that you can control.

Imagine a journey in a hot air balloon: think about taking off, going higher and higher, then looking down on the world passing below before you gently land and step out of the basket.

48 Practise yoga

One of the oldest forms of exercise for both body and mind, yoga originated in ancient India. Yoga combines breathing and meditation with poses. Those who practise it believe it makes them feel healthier and happier.

Taking a break from your walk and doing a spot of yoga outdoors will help connect you even more to your surroundings. The origins of yoga are deeply rooted in nature – in fact, many yoga poses are named after natural elements, such as plants and animals.

Try these basic poses and get closer to nature:

Mountain
Stand with your feet hip-distance apart and your arms hanging down by your sides, palms facing in. Press your feet into the ground, stand up straight and feel strong and tall, like a mountain.

Tree
Balance on your left foot. Slowly lift your right leg and place your foot on the inside of your left leg. Place your hands together and see how long you can hold your balance for. Repeat on the other side.

Snake
Lie on your tummy. Place your hands on the floor, palms down, beneath your shoulders. Gently press into your hands and forearms to lift the top half of your body up. Take few deep breaths, then lower yourself back down.

Here are some other yoga poses for you to research online with the help of a grown-up.

Warrior

Camel

Frog

Lotus

Cow

Fish

Cat

Bridge

GO MOBILE
Make a deck of cards showing the yoga poses you know and take it on your walk. Choose a card and strike a pose!

Tips
49–76

Get creative

Just because you're on your feet, it doesn't mean you can't get hands on! Feel inspired by your surroundings and use things you find in nature to make works of art, crafts and music as you move, or collect items on your walk to get artistic with when you arrive home.

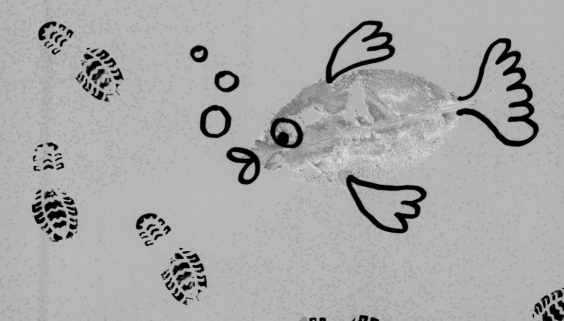

49 Create a nature bracelet

Explore, collect and stick together! Take a roll of tape with you on your walk and make yourself a beautiful, unique bracelet, entirely decorated with nature. Ask a grown-up to help you wrap a piece of tape loosely around your wrist, sticky side out, and simply attach bits and pieces you find on your walk to it. Twigs, leaves, petals, small stones, flower heads, seeds, grass – whatever you like – can all be stuck onto the tape until there's no room left.

Try adding a variety of different coloured flowers and leaves to your bracelet.

50 Make a daisy chain

Wild daisies are a common sight throughout much of the world. If you come across a patch that no-one will mind you picking, thread a few stems together to create a daisy chain, which you can then make into a necklace, bracelet or crown.

You will need:
★ Lots of daisies with long stems
★ A small, pointy twig

How to create a daisy chain

1. Choose a daisy. Near the bottom of its stem, carefully make a small slit with the pointy end of a twig (or with your thumbnail if it's long enough).

2. Pick up a second daisy and delicately thread the stem through the hole you've just made, until it stops at the flower head.

3. Make a hole on the stem of the second daisy, and thread a third daisy through it.

4. Continue until you have a long chain of daisies. Join the ends together by making a second slit in the first daisy and threading the stem of the last daisy back through it.

Daisy chains don't last long, so enjoy them while you can!

MIX IT UP
You don't have to use daisies. Use whatever flowers you like, or even a mixture of different blooms for a more individual look.

62

51 Collect flowers to press

Go on a walk to collect wildflowers that you can take home to press, then make wonderful craft projects from them. Remember to only pick flowers that you know are common and that there are lots of. If you're not sure, don't pick them!

On your walk, you will need:

★ Small scissors
★ Container or small paper bag

Pick and press

1. Pick flowers from late morning onwards. Any earlier in the day and they will be damp with dew.

2. Once picked, put your flowers into a container so they don't get damaged.

3. As soon as you are home, open an old, heavy book and lay a sheet of kitchen paper on the page. Carefully place your flowers on top of the kitchen paper, spreading them out so they don't overlap.

4. Lay another sheet of kitchen paper on top of the flowers. Repeat this process on other pages if you have more flowers.

5. Close the book and move it somewhere out of the way, then pile a few more books on top.

6. After two or three weeks your flowers should be ready. Use them on greetings cards and bookmarks, or use PVA glue to stick them onto a jam jar to create a unique pen pot.

When you get home, you will need:

★ A few old heavy books
★ Kitchen paper or tissue paper

Wildflowers wilt soon after you've picked them, especially on a warm day, so get them home and pressed quickly.

Flat flowerheads work best!

Bees love wildflowers, so if you see one just let it carry on and move somewhere else. Don't swat it away!

52 Create a journey stick

A journey stick, or story stick, is a collection of items gathered on a journey, attached to a stick and used as a memento. If you add the items in order, you can later use the stick as a memory aid to retell the story of your walk.

How to make your journey stick

1. Find a long, thick stick, and wrap a length of string or wool around it, or use elastic bands.

2. As you walk, tuck leaves, twigs, flowers, feathers – basically anything you find on the ground that helps tell the story of your journey – into the string on your stick. Start at one end and work your way along. If you have a pen you can also draw symbols on your stick to describe events and places you've visited.

3. At the end of your journey, you can recall where you went and what happened, as each piece of nature acts as a reminder. Or you could think up a new make-believe story, using the items as prompts.

TOP TIP
Use a nature identification book or app to identify things you find along the way, too.

Everyone's journey will be different, even if they walk along the same path. Compare your stick to other people's. How do they vary?

53 Look for kindness stones

You're on a walk and see something bright out of the corner of your eye. You look closely and realise you have discovered a beautiful hand-painted rock! Sometimes called kindness stones, these rocks are painted and hidden for someone else to find and enjoy. They come in all sizes, and usually show a colourful pattern, a picture or an uplifting, inspirational message.

You could become a kindness stone artist too. You just need a smooth stone or pebble and something to decorate it with.

Make a kindness stone

1. Colour the stone with a base coat of paint. This can be any colour you like. Leave it to dry.

2. Decorate the stone with your design – either a picture or a positive message.

3. Let your stone dry overnight, then paint it with sealer to protect it from the elements. If you don't have any sealer, then a few layers of PVA glue will work too.

4. Spread happiness by choosing a place on your next walk to leave your rock for someone else to find.

54 Make a chalk walk

If you're feeling arty, keep an eye out for soft, crumbly, light-coloured rock that you can draw on the ground with. Design mazes for your walking companions, play hopscotch, create a winding path to follow or make an arrow trail – let your imagination lead you.

You could use your own chalks from home. Just make sure they are natural chalks with no added chemicals, oil or wax, as these aren't good for the environment.

55 Sculpt with nature

Get creative and design yourself a sculpture from the things you find around you. Make your creation while you take a break from walking, or collect pieces to take home with you.

WHAT IS A SCULPTURE?

A sculpture is a 3-D piece of art. It can be made from any material – whatever its creator chooses to use.

Free-standing sculptures

These kinds of sculptures stand on their own and can be viewed from different angles. Stack pebbles, arrange sticks or make a tower of pine cones for all to admire. Take a photo of your art to remember it by, then take it apart and return everything to where you found it.

Make a mandala pattern

The word 'mandala' is a Sanskrit term that means 'circle'. These round patterns feature a design that radiates out from the centre. Using natural materials, start in the middle and create circular patterns as you work your way outwards.

Different coloured leaves work well in a mandala.

Compose a scene

Use natural materials to make a picture on the ground, or collect supplies to create some art when you get home. Your picture can be of whatever you want – let your creativity flow!

What's it all about?

Art isn't just about making something nice for people to look at. It often tells a story or has a message for whoever is looking at it. Maybe your art is themed on a past holiday, a wish for the future or protecting nature and our planet?

Andy Goldsworthy

Andrew Rogers

Nancy Holt

Feel inspired

Delve into the world of environmental art by looking at the work of these artists, all of whom have created sculptures from nature.

Nils-Udo

Robert Smithson

Richard Shilling

Harvey Fite

David Nash

67

56 Nature rubbings

Make some funky art from all the interesting textures you find on your walk! Tree trunks, leaves and stones all have bumpy surfaces that produce great rubbings; all you need is a sheet of paper and a crayon.

You will need:
★ Plain white paper
★ A dark-coloured crayon (if it has a paper covering, peel it off)

How to create your rubbing

- Hunt for a surface with good texture, like the bark of a tree, or a metal sign with bumpy letters on it.
- Lay your paper over the textured area.
- Hold the crayon on its side and rub it across the textured area. Start gently to begin with, then increase the pressure to make the image stronger.
- Take rubbings from different trees and leaves and label them on your picture. How do the results compare?

Add watercolour paint or inks to your crayon rubbing when you get home to make a really colourful design!

Rubbings don't have to be only taken from nature. Look around for patterned ironworks or engraved stones on your walk too. Avoid taking rubbings from old tombstones or ancient buildings without asking permission though — you don't want to damage the stone.

57 Leaf prints

Leaves also make really effective prints. They are perfect for creating greeting cards or framing for homemade wall art. Collect leaves in a variety of different shapes and sizes on your walk, then when you get home, simply use a brush to apply paint to the bumpiest side and print them onto plain paper.

Turn your prints into funny leaf creatures by doodling on eyes, mouths and other features!

58 Paint with nature

Did you know you can actually use nature's own colours to paint with? Natural pigments (colours) were first used thousands of years ago. Cave artists would mix earth, blood and charcoal with animal fat or saliva to create brown, red and black colours for their paintings.

Take a sketchbook, a brush and some water in a jar on your next walk and experiment with what you can find. Crush charcoal with a stone and add a drop of water to make grey, squidge berries (if a grown-up knows they are safe) to make pinks and purples, press the middle of a daisy directly onto the paper to create yellow and paint with sloppy mud for brown. What other colour paint can you discover on your walk?

Take a few containers with you so you can keep the paints separate from one another.

The cave paintings of Baja California, Mexico, are thought to be around 3,500 years old.

Some colours work best made from spices, fruit and vegetables. With a grown-up's help, do some research online and see what paints you can create from food you have at home.

⑤⑨ Get snapping

You don't have to use a smartphone. If you're lucky enough to have your own camera, use that instead.

If you don't own a phone with a camera, someone else in your walking group probably does. Ask if they would be happy for you to borrow their phone, so you can have a go at one of the following photographic activities.

Document your trip

Take pictures at the start and end of your trip, and every few minutes in between, to create a storyboard of your journey. Vary your style – mix close ups with group shots, long-distance views and selfies for an interesting collection of images.

Create optical illusions

Can you make it look like you are holding a famous landmark, or levitating above the ground? Have fun with angles and viewpoints and make your own optical illusions.

70

Organise a competition

Having some sort of competition can be fun if you have more than one camera in the group. Give everyone a topic, such as 'science in nature', 'wildlife at work' or simply a colour theme, and, at the end of your walk, compare the photos you've all taken.

Make googly eyed monsters

Find a couple of light-coloured stones and draw a black circle in the middle of each one in permanent pen. You now have a pair of googly eyes! Place them on various things you see on your walk and bring them to life with your photos.

Add eyes to a letter box, or create a mossy rock monster!

Fill an album with nature pictures

Take snaps of anything interesting you see in nature and create an album of your best pics.

Ask a grown-up to print your photos so you can make a montage.

71

60 Invent your own perfume

Make a lovely scent from items gathered on your walk. Simply collect leaves, blossom, bark or wildflowers that you know aren't protected and that there are plenty of, and leave them in water overnight.

Research which wildflowers in your part of the world give the best scent. For an extra zingy punch, include some fruit peel from your snack box, or find some wild herbs to add.

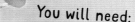

Pour your scent into a bottle or jar and design a label. What will you call yours?

For my Grandma

Ishan's Lavender Breeze

Ishan's Lavender Breeze

How to make perfume

1. Gather your ingredients and put them in a bowl.
2. Pour in just enough water to cover everything. You want to keep the scent strong, so don't add too much.
3. Leave overnight for the scent to infuse the water.

61 Collect petals for confetti

Make confetti for a special occasion – or just to play with your friends. Collect petals on your walk, either from the ground or from flowers that are about to drop them. Once home, cover a baking sheet with a layer of tissue or kitchen paper and spread out the petals. Leave them somewhere warm to dry out for a few days, such as in an airing cupboard.

KEEP IT FRESH
Store your petal confetti in a jar without a lid, so it doesn't sweat.

62 Concoct a magic potion

Spells, potions and all things magical are often linked to nature. Take a jam jar on your next walk and collect the ingredients you need to create your own special potion. You could use it to perform a spell – perhaps one that makes you run fast or turns things invisible...

WARNING!
Your potion is for looking at and playing with only. Don't drink it!

Good magic potion ingredients

- ★ Moss
- ★ Shells
- ★ Dried leaves
- ★ Dew
- ★ Dandelion seeds
- ★ Flowers
- ★ Tiny pebbles

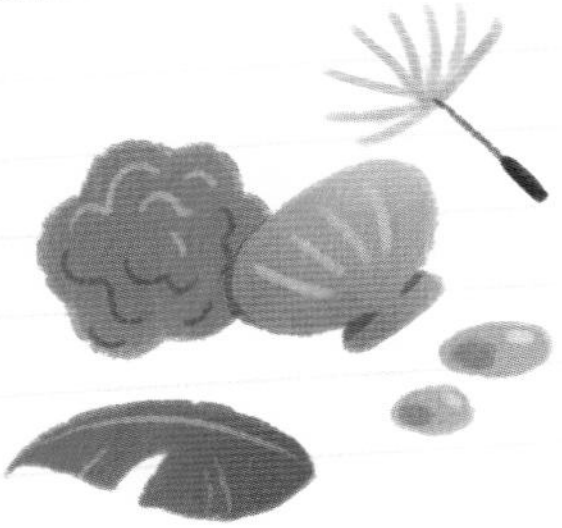

If you want to collect a few ingredients to make more potions at home, take a few different containers to keep everything separate.

Once you have found all your ingredients, look for a little hollowed-out tree stump or bowl-shaped rock filled with rainwater. You can use these to mix your potion in, for added magic.

Add flower petals to your potion for extra colour and scent.

Why not use nature to make a magic wand to go with your potion?

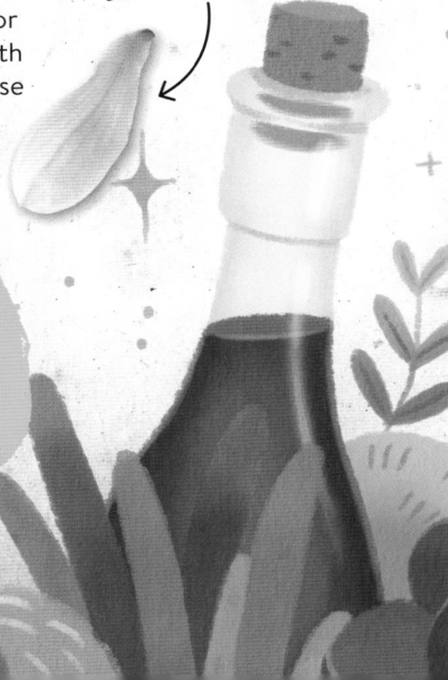

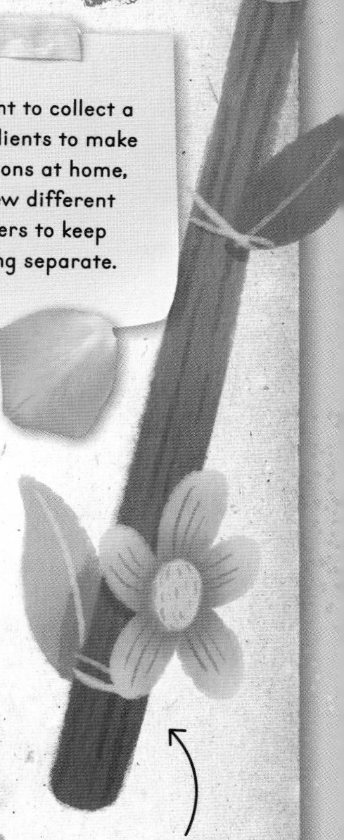

ABRACADABRA!
All the best magic potions have a spell to go with them. Use your imagination to write a spell of your own, then sprinkle the potion while you're reading it aloud.

63 Cloud gazing

Take a moment to lie back and relax, look up at the clouds as they roll across the sky and let your imagination take over. What crazy things can you see?

A puppy? A turtle? Or a whale spouting water?

An elephant? A dinosaur? Or a monkey wearing a top hat?

Cumulus clouds are the best type for cloud gazing adventures. These are the clouds you usually get on a warm, sunny day. They're white and fluffy, like cotton wool, and they keep changing shape, which means one minute you could see a grizzly bear carrying an umbrella, and the next minute a lion wearing boxing gloves!

Cloud gaze with someone else. Do you agree on what you can see in the clouds, or are you each imagining different scenes?

Make up a story with the characters you see. How about taking a photo and editing it in an app to make it look even more like your make-believe character?

64 Hunt for hidden faces

Have you ever felt like a tree is watching your every move? Or that a rock is groaning at your fashion sense? Keep your eyes peeled for funny faces and take photo evidence to prove to your friends and family that tree beasts and rock monsters DO exist!

Look for faces in human-made things too, such as doorbells, letter boxes and fire hydrants.

Make a photo collection of all the faces you find.

65 Make a nature creature

How about creating a friendly bat to keep you company on your journey? Or a creepy critter to scare your friends with? Pack some modelling clay and use natural materials you find on your walk to create your very own nature creature.

You will need:
★ Sticks, moss, seed pods, leaves, flowers and various other natural materials
★ Modelling clay
★ Your imagination!

TOP TIP
Use modelling clay to stick everything together.

75

66 Hunt for mythical creatures

Could there be dragons lurking in the depths of the forest, a troll taking a snooze under the bridge you are walking over, or fairies living among the long grasses of the riverbank?

Can you spot any signs? Use your imagination and you'll probably start finding evidence for magical creatures all around you.

Troll prints?

A unicorn's horn?

Could this be the empty egg shell of a baby dragon?

A mermaid's tail scales?

A cheeky pixie's catapult?

The home of a goblin family?

A fairy's necklace?

An elf's shield?

A leprechaun's hammock?

Have dragons been sharpening their claws here?

The baby teeth of an ogre?

Can you discover any more?

67 Play with a stick

With a bit of imagination, a stick can be so many things. What will yours be – a magic wand, a sword, a giant pencil, or something else entirely?

A lightsaber?

A wand?

A fishing rod?

A hiking stick?

A microphone?

68 Whizz your way home

Make yourself a magic broomstick and zoom off to your destination.

You will need:
★ One long, straight branch
★ Lots of small, thin twigs, roughly the same length (snap some down to size if you need to)
★ String or a rubber band

How to make a broomstick

1. Bunch your thin twigs together, lining them up at one end.

2. Place them around the end of the long branch, and tie string tightly or use a rubber band to hold them in place. Push more twigs in if the string or rubber band is feeling slack.

3. Off you go! If you want your broomstick to last longer, use PVA glue when you get home to hold the twigs together more securely.

69 Create a wind streamer

Take some lengths of ribbon, old material or wool on your walk and transform a long stick into a colourful wind streamer! Simply find a chunky stick that feels good to hold, then tie your lengths of ribbon, material or wool to one end. That's it!

Can you create patterns with the ribbons as you walk? Or even make up a dance?

Choose a breezy day to get the most fun out of this activity!

70 Hone your slingshot skills

Hunt for a strong Y-shaped stick and, along with a thick elastic band, you'll have all you need to create a slingshot.

Use moss or scrunched up paper, if you have some, as your ammunition, but be sure to pick it all up off the ground when you finish.

Test your aim and do some target practice exercises as you walk. Can you hit a tree trunk from a metre (3 ft) away? If that's easy, move back and try from a further distance. How accurate is your aim now?

You will need:
★ A Y-shaped stick
★ A thick elastic band, cut once so you have a strip

How to make a basic slingshot

1. Make sure your stick is sturdy enough. Press the prongs backwards while holding the handle to check it won't break.
2. Tie the ends of your elastic around each of the prongs.
3. Place your ammunition in the centre of the elastic, pull back and release!

SAFETY FIRST!
★ Don't fire at people or animals.
★ Only use soft materials as your ammunition. Never be tempted to fire stones as you could really hurt someone or damage property.

Remember to take all materials home with you when you have finished with them!

71 Make a twig raft

If your journey takes you through woods and near a stream, collect sticks along the way and make a miniature raft to set sail.

How to create your raft

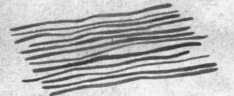

① Lay your 12 sticks together with the edges lined up.

Use biodegradable string in case your raft sails away.

② Using string, tie a secure knot at one end of the first stick, about 2 cm (1 in) from the end.

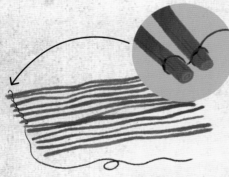

③ Wrap the string around the second stick, then tie a knot to attach it to the first stick. Continue to work your way along, tying knots around all 12 sticks, then cut the string. Try not to leave any gaps between the sticks if you can.

④ Repeat steps 2 and 3 at the other end of the raft.

80

The two thicker sticks need to be laid in the opposite direction to the other sticks, as shown.

You could create a passenger from natural materials to travel on your raft. See page 75 for some ideas.

❺ Lay the two thicker sticks near the string at each end of the raft. Snap them if you need to, so they are the same length as the raft's width.

❻ Use the string to tie knots around the thicker sticks, fixing them securely to the raft.

MAKE IT YOUR OWN
Use petals and leaves to personalise your raft and make it stand out.

❼ Tear a small hole at each end of the leaf and thread the thin twig through it, as shown, to create a mast and sail.

❽ Turn your raft over so the two thicker sticks are on the underside. Gently push the mast between two of the sticks, so it stands upright.

❾ Tie a length of string to your raft, then take it for a test sail.

Try sailing your raft in a shallow pool of water first. Does it float? Is it ready for a bigger journey? Make any changes you need to before launching it for real.

TAKE CARE
Water is dangerous. Only float your raft where it's shallow and remember to be super-careful and sensible at all times.

72 Become a storyteller

Entertain yourselves by working together to tell a thrilling adventure story. You could choose to include traditional fairytale characters, such as knights, princesses, witches, magic frogs and dragons, or create your own truly unique tale.

Set a theme before you start and make up a story with the rest of your group, taking it in turns to say a sentence or two. If you know anything about the history of the area you are walking through, you could use this as a starting point. Locations along your walk could set the scene, and people through history could be your characters. Or base your story in the present day – or even the future – and cast people around you in the leading roles. Where will your tale take you?

How to tell the perfect tale

Being a great storyteller isn't just about the story you tell. Use expression, emotion and gestures to add drama and interest. Be enthusiastic, using your tone of voice, eyes, facial expressions and body movements to bring your story to life!

GO SOLO

Once you've mastered the basics of storytelling in a group, try creating one yourself. Entertain your walking companions with your very own gripping tale.

73 Write a poem

Feel inspired by your surroundings and write a poem about where you are.

Poems don't have to rhyme, but they can be fun if they do. What kind of poem would you like to write on your next walk?

Limerick

The lines of a limerick follow a pattern, so that the first, second and fifth lines all have the same rhythm and rhyme. The third and fourth lines also rhyme with each other, but are shorter. Limericks are usually funny and are often about people.

> There once was a young lad called Will
> Who hiked to the top of a hill
> He forgot his map
> And couldn't get back
> So to this day there he is still

It doesn't matter if you don't have perfect rhyming words, as long as you have the right rhythm.

Haiku

Originating from Japan, these short poems consist of just 17 syllables: five in the first line, seven in the second, and five in the third (last) line. Traditionally, they would have been written about the author's surroundings, or the changing seasons.

Acrostic poem

In an acrostic poem, the first letter in each line spells a word. This word is what the poem is all about.

> **W**ith much excitement, we set off early
> **A** loop around the lake, our latest challenge
> **L**ittle legs start to tire, energy levels wane
> **K**eep up, everyone!

5 syllables

> Everlasting heat
> Gives way to cool autumn mist
> Goodbye summer days

7 syllables

5 syllables

WHAT'S A SYLLABLE?

Syllables are like beats in a word. To count syllables, count how many beats the words make.

83

74 Make music

Did you know you can get musical with all kinds of things you find in nature? In ancient times, instruments were made from materials such as animal skin, bones and wood, and they would have been played for enjoyment or as part of a ceremony.

Thankfully, you don't need to use animal skin or bones to make music while out walking! Create one of these instruments and let rhythm and melody take you on a unique journey...

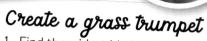

Reed instruments, like the clarinet, oboe and saxophone, all make noise in a similar way to a grass trumpet!

Create a grass trumpet

1. Find the widest blade of grass you can and, holding your hands together, position it between the outer edges of your thumbs.

2. Press your thumbs together, making sure the grass is being held taught and flat.

3. Blow between your thumbs. The grass should vibrate, sounding a bit like a trumpet.

4. Make a hole in the blade of grass for a louder noise!

75 Compose a marching song

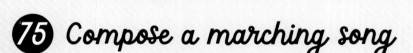

Marching songs are a great way to get everyone moving with purpose – and they're lots of fun, too. One person is the leader, who sings (or shouts) the lines of the song. The rest of the 'troop' repeat the words, to the same beat and melody. Print the lyrics to well-known marching songs before your head out, or simply make up your own.

"Everywhere we go..."

"Everywhere we go..."

Feel the beat

1. Look for two strong sticks, about 30 cm (12 in) long.
2. Use them as drumsticks, tapping out a rhythm.

Try hitting your drumsticks on different surfaces to get a variety of sounds. Which sounds best — a tree trunk, a stone wall or a plastic lunchbox?

Shake those maracas

1. Gather a selection of small stones and put them inside an old plastic bottle or sandwich tub.
2. Fasten the lid and shake!

What happens if you use big stones instead of little stones? Does it sound different?

What other noises can you make? Try replicating sounds of nature, birdsong or animal noises. Can you make instruments out of other things?

76 Create a band

Now that you know how to make music from nature, you can create a band with your walking buddies! With one person on drums, someone else shaking a beat, another playing the grass trumpet and someone on vocals, you could recreate one of your favourite songs.

**Tips
77–101**

Play games

It's time to hike up the fun factor! Use your imagination and adapt some well-known games to play in the great outdoors. Get energetic with your friends and family as you all search, race, hide and seek, or flex those mental muscles with a word or memory game. Who will take on your challenge and come out on top?

77 Play 'I spy'

If there's one game everyone is familiar with, it's 'I spy'. It's a classic! But did you know there are lots of different ways to play it? Ditch the traditional letter version and try one of these instead.

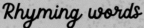

Rhyming words
I spy something that rhymes with...

Textures
I spy something bumpy...

Colours
I spy something pink...

I spy something tiny, worth 5 points.

Shapes
I spy something round...

Numbers
I spy three of these...

Measurements
I spy something about 5 cm (2 in) long...

Ladybird?

Or mix it up and do a selection as you play!

ADD POINTS
Give each item a points value and keep score — the harder you think it will be to guess the item, the greater the number of points you should give it.

BEAT THE CLOCK
Include a time limit to make it harder.

78 Act it out

The popular game of charades can be played anywhere! At the top of a mountain, on a coastal walk or in the depths of a forest – it really doesn't matter where you are. You can even play it on the move, too.

How to play

Charades is a guessing game in which one player acts out a word or phrase without speaking, and the rest of the players try to guess what it is.

❶ The first player begins by thinking of something they'd like to act out. It could be a book, a television programme, a film, a song title or something else entirely.

❷ The player tells everyone which category they have chosen. Note: this is the only speaking the player will do – from this point on, no words are allowed!

❸ The player holds up the same number of fingers as there are words in the phrase. If they are acting out the film *The Wizard of Oz*, for example, they would hold up four fingers.

❹ Once everyone has understood how many words are in the phrase, the player tells the team which word they are acting out first by holding up the matching number of fingers. For example, they would hold up two fingers if they were going to act out the word 'wizard'.

❺ Next, the player describes the number of syllables by resting the corresponding number of fingers on their forearm.

❻ Whenever anyone gets a word right, the player points at them and nods.

If you're feeling confident, you could try acting out the entire title in one go!

TEAM UP!

If there are enough of you, divide into two teams. Each team chooses a player to mime to their teammates, and they each have three minutes to get as many right as they can. Whichever team guesses the most is the winner!

Sounds like 'bunny'?

You can also act out words that rhyme with the word the players need to guess. Just tug your ear before acting it out (tugging your ear means 'sounds like...').

⟨79⟩ Search and scramble

This is a great game to lift energy levels! Decide on one person to be the leader. The leader sets a challenge for all players to find something in particular and race to bring it back to them. The first player to return to the leader with the correct item wins.

BE KIND

Remember to not damage plants or property, and to put things back where you found them.

Here are some ideas to start you off...

| A twig shaped like a Y | A small grey feather | A symmetrical leaf | A red leaf | A stripy shell |

Not every item has to be from nature. How about including some of these ideas? You may need to think more creatively and ask some of your group for help...

A pen

A black shoelace

A coin

An empty food packet

PHOTOGRAPHIC EVIDENCE

If everyone has access to a smartphone, ask each player to take a photo instead of collecting the item. This should give you a bigger amount of things to choose from, as you can include things in the distance or items that can't be moved from their location.

80 Who can find the biggest, the smallest, the thinnest...

Who can find the biggest pine cone? The smallest pebble? The thinnest twig? Play this game in the same way as 'search and scramble', with one player as the leader.

It's best to introduce a time limit – one or two minutes should be about right – otherwise the more competitive players in the group will just keep hunting!

81 Go on a number hunt

There are numbers all over the place, even in rural areas. Starting at 1 and spotting digits as you walk, how far can you count? Work as a team and look for signs, notices, ironworks (such as drains and manhole covers), way markers, car registration plates, shop windows and bus stops displaying numbers. Set yourselves a target at the start of your walk, or just see how far you can go.

PLAY BY THE RULES

In this game, the numbers have to be found as standalone figures. For example, if you're looking for the number 2 you can't use the 2 out of the number 12.

82 Hunt high, hunt low

Who doesn't love a scavenger hunt? Create a list of items to find on your outdoor adventure and give a copy to each person, along with a pen or pencil, at the start of your walk. As your walking buddies spot the things on the list, they tick them off.

There are many scavenger hunts online for you to choose from, or you could create one of your own. Just think about where you're heading and the season you're in, and select things you think you might spot. Make sure to put a few trickier items in there too!

Customise it

Adapt your scavenger hunt to your surroundings. For a walk in a built-up area, you'll need to think up some different things. How about these suggestions?

- Someone drinking coffee
- A red car
- A traffic warden
- Someone pushing a pram
- A dog being taken for a walk
- A round window
- A pigeon
- A street sign
- A pizzeria
- Someone playing music
- An empty bus stop
- Someone talking on their phone

You can still include some nature-themed things too, like insects or plants.

SEARCH FOR THESE ITEMS:

A pine cone ☐
Two differently shaped leaves ☐
A flat pebble ☐
A butterfly ☐
A yellow flower ☐
Something fluffy ☐
Something painted ☐
A plant with thorns ☐
A stick longer than you ☐
A feather ☐
A spotty rock ☐
Moss ☐
A ladybird ☐

Work individually, in pairs or in teams if there are enough of you. Just remember to take enough pens or pencils for everyone!

Your scavenger hunt doesn't have to be a simple list of things to spot. Try some of these ideas too...

Colour fun

Instead of a list of different items to spot, make a list of colours, patterns and textures. Leave an area next to each one for an answer. When someone sees something that matches, they write down what they spotted in the space.

Listen out!

How about a sounds-based scavenger hunt, in which all players have to listen out for different noises? You could ask each player to record the sounds on a phone as proof!

Assign points

Take your scavenger hunt to the next level by adding points and a time-frame. Give higher points for more difficult-to-find items. Once the time has run out, tot up the scores to see who the winner is.

Anagram hunt

Make it even trickier by providing the items to spot as anagrams so players have to unscramble the letters first! Who will be the first to find a SPEWBIDER, a BRADYLID or a DYLANFROG? (Find the answers to these anagrams below.)

For some scavenger hunts, players collect items. If you're playing a collecting game just be sure what you are gathering is safe, plentiful and doesn't belong to others!

Give each player a colour chart or painted egg carton and ask them to find items to match.

Anagrams
SPIDERWEB, LADYBIRD and DRAGONFLY

83 Hide and find

Only using the words 'hotter' and 'colder', can you describe how close someone is to discovering an item that's been hidden along the route?

One person hides an item up ahead, while the others look away or close their eyes. The players work together to try and find it, while the person who hid the object says 'hotter' as they get closer to the hiding place, and 'colder' as they move further away. Whoever finds the item first gets to hide it in the next round. However, there's a catch – if all players walk past the hiding place without finding the item, it's game over!

84 Get dribbling

Master your soccer skills with a pine cone or a conker. See how long you can stay in control as you dribble it along your route. It won't be long before your fellow walkers start joining in, either with their own 'ball', or by trying to tackle you for yours!

Falling to the ground in autumn, pine cones contain the seeds of pine trees. At other times of the year, when it's harder to find pine cones, you could use a small stone or pebble – they make excellent mini-footballs too.

NOT FOR DOGS!

Don't play this game with a conker if you have a furry companion with you. Conkers are just the right size for a dog to choke on, and they are poisonous.

85 Create mini-races

Challenge your companions to a series of races – and perhaps compete for special nature-themed medals! Put your heads together and come up with a series of different competitions you can do along the route.

Agree on a starting point and finish line before you start.

Here are some ideas:

★ Hopping race

★ Running backwards race

★ Three-legged race, in pairs
  (use a scarf to tie your legs)

★ Balancing race (with a piece of fruit from your snack box – or a small pebble – on your head)

★ Piggyback race

Non-racing activities

You could include other events too. Place a stick on the ground as the starting point for a long-jump competition, or see who can jump to reach a branch of a tree.

Try making your own winners medals!

Can you make up any games or events of your own?

95

86 Create a human chain

This is a great game if there are a few of you on your walk. It's a bit like tag or 'It', with one person (who is 'It') trying to chase and catch other members of the group. When someone is caught, they join hands with the person who caught them, and together they continue to chase the other players.

The chain gets longer and longer (and more difficult to manage!) until there is only one person left to catch – this person is the winner and becomes 'It' in the next round.

STICK TOGETHER
Everyone must try their hardest to keep holding hands so the chain doesn't break!

You moved!

Stand as still as a statue when the leader turns around.

87 Freeze!

Choose one player to be the leader. The leader walks about 15 m (50 ft) ahead of the rest of the group. Everyone else tries to catch up. However, if the leader turns around, everyone must stand still. If the leader spots someone moving, that person is out of the game. The winner is the first person to catch up with the leader.

88 Play 'floor is lava'

'Floor is lava in 5, 4, 3, 2, 1...' If you've ever heard those words (or said them yourself) you'll know what comes next – everyone pretends that the floor is turning into fiery, hot molten rock and tries to get somewhere 'safe' before the countdown reaches zero. This means stepping or climbing onto something so your feet are off the ground, such as a wall, a large rock or a park bench.

This isn't really an organised game with a start and finish; it's just dropped into conversation every now and then – ideally when everyone is least expecting it!

Hi!

89 Say g'day

It's nice to smile and say 'hi'! How many 'hi's', 'hellos' or 'g'days' can you give and receive on your next walk? It might not sound like much, but this simple gesture can spread a lot of happiness!

You could make it into a game, if you like, by earning points if people say hello back. Either play with a friend, taking it in turns to see who gets the most replies, or play solo and record your score each time you go out.

Morning!

Hello!

G'day!

Make sure you always have a grown-up with you when you're talking to people you don't know.

97

90 Follow the leader

Choose one person to be leader. They head out in front of the group and perform an action of their choice as they walk, such as clapping, nodding or hopping. Everyone following has to mimic what the leader does, no matter how embarrassing!

Make it trickier by tying the action in with the number of paces walked. For example, clicking fingers after walking four paces, or doing a star jump every ten steps. Can everyone work out what they are meant to be doing, and when?

Swap leaders as frequently as you want. For an extra challenge, each new leader could continue what the previous leader did, adding their own action to it. You might get some funny looks from other passers-by, but it's all good fun!

Make the actions as silly as you like. How about doing an elephant impression, picking your nose or wobbling like a jelly as you walk?

Hmm, I'm not sure that looks like an elephant. You're out!

FRIENDLY COMPETITION
Make it into a game. Those who don't follow the leader's actions (or follow them incorrectly) are 'out' and the last person remaining becomes the new leader.

98

91 Change your pace

Walking, skipping, jogging, running – how do you like to get from A to B? One person is the leader, and they shout instructions for everyone to follow on how to travel from one place to the next. If you're feeling energetic, make it into a race each time!

How creative and silly can you get?

Sprint to the bridge.

Gallop to the lamppost.

Bunny-hop to the bench.

Waddle to the café.

Moonwalk to the end of the path.

92 Do whatever Simon says

Don't worry, you can still play 'Simon says' if you don't have someone called Simon in your walking group! One person is chosen to be 'Simon', whose aim is to get everyone out as quickly as possible. 'Simon' calls out commands for the rest of the group to follow, starting each sentence with 'Simon says'. If a phrase doesn't start with 'Simon says', the group can ignore the command. If someone follows the command when they shouldn't, or doesn't follow the command when they should, they are out!

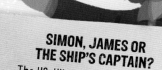

SIMON, JAMES OR THE SHIP'S CAPTAIN?

The US, UK and Australia all play Simon Says, along with many other countries. But not everyone in the world listens to 'Simon'. In France, the commands are given by 'Jacques' (James); in China, it's 'the teacher' giving orders; and, in Japan, everyone does what 'the ship's captain' says!

93 Hide, then seek

One of the oldest games in the world, Hide and Seek is still popular with children today. It's so well-known, there are likely to be very few people who have never played it! But did you know there are many different ways to play?

EARLY HIDE AND SEEK

One of the first people to write about Hide and Seek was a Greek writer called Julius Pollux. In the 2nd century BCE, he described a game called *Apodidraskinda*, which had exactly the same rules as the game played today.

The classic version

You probably already know how to play Hide and Seek, but just in case you don't, here are the rules:

1. Choose one player to be the seeker.

2. The seeker covers their eyes and counts to 20 (or another agreed number) while everyone else hides.

3. Once they have counted to 20, the seeker calls 'Ready or not, here I come!'

4. Everyone stays really still and quiet in their hiding spot until they are found.

5. The first person that the seeker finds will then become the seeker in the next round. The last person to be found is the winner.

Hide, seek, move

Play by these rules and you can change your hiding place to trick the seeker! Players hide as usual but, if they feel the seeker is getting close, they can run to a new hiding place. They just have to be careful they don't get spotted while on the move!

Hide and Seek works best with at least three players.

Team up

In this version of the game, as players are found, they join the seeker and help them look for other people who are hiding.

Sardines

This is a bit like Hide and Seek in reverse, as one person hides while all the other players seek. When a seeker finds the hiding player, they join them in the same hiding space. The game continues until only one seeker remains.

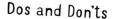

Dos and Don'ts

Regardless of which version you're playing, set a few ground rules before you start to make the game run more smoothly.

★ <u>Do</u> make sure everyone knows where is out of bounds, so no one wanders off.

★ <u>Don't</u> hide anywhere unsafe.

★ <u>Don't</u> trespass on private property.

★ <u>Do</u> set a time limit for looking.

★ <u>Do</u> agree on a phrase to use when the game is over, so anyone still hiding knows they can make themselves visible again.

Jailbreak

In this game, when players are found they have to go to 'jail' (a separate agreed area). The seeker's aim is to get all players in jail. However, players who haven't yet been found can free those in jail by sneaking out from their hiding spot and tagging those in jail while the seeker isn't looking. If they manage to do this without being caught, they all run to new hiding places and the game continues.

TELL A GROWN-UP
Let the adults you are walking with know what you're playing, so they don't worry where everyone is. Better still, ask them to join in!

101

94 Make games from natural materials

What games can you make from nature? Play to pass the time while you're taking a rest or eating a snack, then continue your journey!

Noughts and crosses

Either scratch lines into the ground, or lay four sticks down to make a grid. Then use two different types of item in place of the noughts and crosses, such as pebbles and shells if you are on the beach, or leaves and small twigs if you are on a woodland walk.

Pebble toss

This is a great game for the beach. Dig a hole in the sand, and give five small pebbles to each player. Take it in turns to throw your stones into the hole. Whoever gets the most in wins.

What do you feel?

Collect a selection of items of various sizes and textures. Put them into an empty rucksack or sandwich box and ask others to feel what's inside and guess what the items are. Give them a point for each correct answer. Who can guess the most?

Draw a line in the sand for players to stand behind. Grown-ups could go further back!

Dig a hole in the sand big enough for the pebbles to land in.

Think of some board games you might have at home. Can you recreate any of your favourites?

Board game

Draw a board design into sand or dusty ground, then use pebbles, shells or leaves as counters.

VIRTUAL DICE
Use a dice-rolling app if your game requires it.

Memory game

Lay ten or so different items on the ground. Ask the rest of your group to try and memorise the items for around 20 seconds, then ask them to look away. Remove one item and ask them to look again. Who will be the first to figure out which item has been removed?

Make it harder for the other players by rearranging the remaining items!

Draughts

Scratch a grid into the ground – eight squares wide by eight squares high. Decide on two different materials to use as draughts (you'll need 12 of each) and lay them out in place on the grid.

You can use the same grid for snakes and ladders!

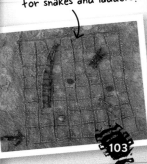

If you don't know how to play draughts, check the rules online or ask a grown-up to teach you.

103

95 Play alphabet categories

Exercise your brain as well as your body by playing a fun word game. This one is simple enough to be enjoyed by players of all ages!

How to play

1. Everyone agrees on a leader, plus a category, such as countries, names or creatures.
2. The leader runs through the alphabet in their head.
3. Someone says 'STOP' and the leader tells everyone which letter of the alphabet they have landed on.
4. Everyone tries to think of something belonging to the category agreed at the start of the game. Their answer must begin with the letter the leader stopped on.
5. Each player says their answer in turn, continuing until somebody can't go. If everyone has given a correct answer, the players carry on giving more answers until someone gets stuck.
6. The person who got stuck goes first next time, using a new letter. This could either be in the same category, or a new one.

96 Play the word association game

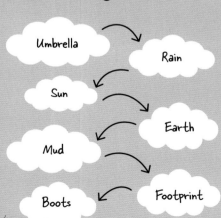

This game gets you thinking quickly! No 'ums' or 'errs' allowed!

How to play

1. The first player says a word. Any word will do, but nouns (names of things) usually work best.

2. The next player says a word that relates to the word the first player said, then play moves on to the next player.

3. Play continues until someone either takes longer than a few seconds to say their answer, says 'um' or 'err', repeats an answer that's already been said or says a word that clearly doesn't relate to the previous one.

97 Test your memory skills

Play a game with your walking buddies in which everyone adds something to a list. How many items can you remember before it feels like your brain will explode?

This is based on the classic game 'Grandma went to market', but you can change the person and the setting. You could even make it about you and your journey!

EASY AS ABC

Can you think up answers in alphabetical order? It might make it more of a challenge to come up with each item, but it can help you remember the order of the answers.

How to play

1. The first player begins by saying the opening line, along with the first item on the list. For example, this could be 'Auntie Donna went to a party and wore some brightly coloured earrings'.

2. The next player repeats what the first player said, and adds an item of their own. For example, 'Auntie Donna went to a party and wore some brightly coloured earrings and sparkly shoes'.

3. The next player continues. 'Auntie Donna went to a party and wore some brightly coloured earrings, sparkly shoes and a pirate costume'.

4. The game continues until someone can't remember the list, or gets the order wrong.

While out walking I saw...

an ant
a beautiful flower
a chocolate ice cream
a duck
an empty eggshell
a field
... and a glove!

PLAY TOGETHER

This game doesn't have to be competitive. It's just as much fun to all work together to try and remember as many items as possible, helping each other out when you need to.

98 Name that tune

How's your pitch and tempo? Pick a song and hum it. Can anyone else guess what it is? Once you've mastered the basics, try one of the following variations.

Try picking a theme for your song that everyone in your group loves, such as movie soundtracks, musicals or animated films.

Say that tune

As an extra challenge for your listeners, speak the words instead of humming the tune. Guessing the song when you can't hear the tune is harder than it sounds!

Sing it slowly

Take your time and slow the song right down. It will make guessing much harder!

Guess the intro

Use a music app to play the first few seconds of a song and see if anyone can recognise it.

99 Play twenty questions

This classic game is perfect for long walks, long car journeys or long checkout queues, and it's really easy to play.

One player thinks of something – anything – and lets the rest of the group know whether they are thinking of a person, a place or a thing. The other players are allowed to ask up to twenty questions between them before they can guess what the player is thinking of. Each question can only be answered with a 'yes' or 'no', so everyone has to really think how best to ask the question to get a useful answer!

100 Practise your interview technique

How well do you know the rest of your walking gang? Quiz others in your group about their life, including their interests, likes and dislikes. It's good to talk!

You could also play one of these games to help you get to know everyone better. You might discover that you have more in common than you realise!

Do you prefer...

This is a great game for finding out more about other people's personalities. Take two contrasting ideas and ask your friends or family members which they prefer. You might be surprised by some of their answers! Are their answers the same as the ones you would give?

The yes/no game

Set a time limit – a minute is usually about right – and quiz someone in your group about their life. They have to answer as truthfully as possible, but aren't allowed to say the words 'yes' or 'no'. It's trickier than it sounds!

Maybe?

I think so?

Yes? Argh!

Summer or winter?

Pool or beach?

Staying in or going out?

Apples or bananas?

101 Be a litter champion

Challenge the rest of your group to a competition with a very worthwhile outcome! Each person takes an old plastic bag on your walk and tries to be the first to fill it with rubbish. Ask if you can borrow litter pickers from your local council, library or community centre and leave the area you're walking in even more beautiful than it was when you started out on your journey.

TAKE CARE!
Never pick up sharp objects like broken glass with your hands.

Ticklist

How many of the 101 tips in this book have you completed? Tick them off as you go!

○ #1   Learn to read a map

○ #2   Use a compass

○ #3   Plan an interesting route

○ #4   Discover history

○ #5   Keep a walking journal

○ #6   Get measuring

○ #7   Look closely

○ #8   Spot patterns in nature

○ #9   Take on a teeny-tiny challenge

○ #10 Collect and dissect

○ #11 Build a den

○ #12 Wildlife watch

○ #13 Listen for the birdie

○ #14 Become an animal detective

○ #15 Identify tree types

○ #16 Shake a tree

○ #17 Age a tree

○ #18 Explore a watery world

○ #19 Spot animal homes

○ #20 Identify clouds

○ #21 Become a geologist

○ #22 Go on a fossil hunt

○ #23 Watch the Sun set

○ #24 Go on a bat hunt

○ #25 Torch walk

○ #26 Go stargazing

○ #27 Study the Moon's phases

○ #28 Hike up a hill

○ #29 Roll down a grassy slope

○ #30 Let a coin decide the way

○ #31 Admire the scenery

○ #32 Climb a tree

○ #33 Hug a tree

○ #34 Make a tree swing

○ #35 Create an obstacle course

○ #36 Geocaching

○ #37 Learn the art of trailblazing

○ #38 Count your steps

○ #39 Stop and shop

○ #40 Feed the ducks

○ #41 Make and fly a kite

○ #42 Eat in the fresh air

○ #43 Race sticks

○ #44 Make a stone bounce

○ #45 Have fun with shadows

○ #46 Slow down and use your senses

○ #47 Meditate

○ #48 Practise yoga

○ #49 Create a nature bracelet

○ #50 Make a daisy chain

- O #51 Collect flowers to press
- O #52 Create a journey stick
- O #53 Look for kindness stones
- O #54 Make a chalk walk
- O #55 Sculpt with nature
- O #56 Nature rubbings
- O #57 Leaf prints
- O #58 Paint with nature
- O #59 Get snapping
- O #60 Invent your own perfume
- O #61 Collect petals for confetti
- O #62 Concoct a magic potion
- O #63 Cloud gazing
- O #64 Hunt for hidden faces
- O #65 Make a nature creature
- O #66 Hunt for mythical creatures
- O #67 Play with a stick
- O #68 Whizz your way home
- O #69 Create a wind streamer
- O #70 Hone your slingshot skills
- O #71 Make a twig raft
- O #72 Become a storyteller
- O #73 Write a poem
- O #74 Make music
- O #75 Compose a marching song
- O #76 Create a band

- O #77 Play 'I spy'
- O #78 Act it out
- O #79 Search and scramble
- O #80 Who can find the biggest, the smallest, the thinnest...
- O #81 Go on a number hunt
- O #82 Hunt high, hunt low
- O #83 Hide and find
- O #84 Get dribbling
- O #85 Create mini-races
- O #86 Create a human chain
- O #87 Freeze!
- O #88 Play 'floor is lava'
- O #89 Say g'day
- O #90 Follow the leader
- O #91 Change your pace
- O #92 Do whatever Simon says
- O #93 Hide, then seek
- O #94 Make games from natural materials
- O #95 Play alphabet categories
- O #96 Play the word association game
- O #97 Test your memory skills
- O #98 Name that tune
- O #99 Play twenty questions
- O #100 Practise your interview technique
- O #101 Be a litter champion

My walking record

You could make a note of your favourite walks. Use this as a template to create your own walking journal.

Was it a hilly hike or a stroll along the coast? Or were you on holiday, exploring a new city or town?

You can record distance using a phone app.

Date	Location	Type of walk	Distance